BEST
YORKSHIRE
TALES

COLLECTED FROM "DALESMAN"

Dalesman Publishing Company Ltd
Stable Courtyard, Broughton Hall,
Skipton, North Yorkshire BD23 3AZ

First published 1993
Reprinted in this format 1999

© Dalesman Publishing Company Ltd

Cover illustration by Silvey Jex

A British Library Cataloguing in Publication record
is available for this book

ISBN 1 85568 171 4

Printed by Amadeus Press, Huddersfield

CONTENTS

RURAL WAYS

I was walking one morning along a Pennine summit when I saw an old man mending a drystone wall. It was a glorious day; the hills shone green near at hand, blue in the distance. I nodded to the old chap and said: "Fine morning." He gave me glance of scorn and said witheringly: "Well, don't let's get into a lather about it."

Phyllis Bentley

I took a temporary teaching post in a remote Dales school where fifteen children shared one small classroom. Nature walks helped to relieve congestion. On one occasion, hoping to instil a little arithmetic into the five year old beside me, I enquired: "How many sheep can you count in that field?" A long pause. "Well, Johnnie?" Johnnie looked up with an air of pitying superiority: "Them's moan sheep. Them's bluddy tups."

Winifred Haward

I was walking down the long hill from Dent station when I met a farm lad. After a moment of conversation, and without any devious thought, I asked: "Where would we be if we kept on walking?" The lad scratched his head and replied: "Well, I reckon you'd be coming down this 'ere hill, for they do tell me that t'world is round."

John Foster Beaver

I recall a hot, sunny Sunday when the whole of Wensleydale was shimmering in the heat. My Land Rover was parked in the shade of a high wall. Suddenly the peace was shattered. Standing imprisoned in a large, square, wire-mesh litter basket, on a foot or so of assorted rubbish, was a small, smelly child, whose outstretched hands barely touched the rims of the basket. The sun shone fiercely on the child's head.

Questioning the child brought no information. Ten long minutes went by, and the child's continuous screams were finally answered: "What are you doing with my John?" she demanded. "How dare you take him out of his litter basket? I put him in there to be safe."

Norman Crossley

**"Just three more miles and we should be in sight
of Malham Tarn..."**

In my days as Bishop of Bradford, my wife and I had been out for a country walk. I was dressed in an old pair of grey trousers and an open shirt. As we neared home I said: "Let's buy some crumpets for tea."

We came to a little shop. I poked my head round the corner and said: "Any crumpets?" The lady of the shop called out to her husband: "Albert, do you want any crumpets?" In reply to which he called back: "No thanks, not today."

We didn't get our crumpets but we did get a good laugh.

Dr Donald Coggan

A country postman was so dedicated to his job that he had never taken a holiday for 20 years. His friends said that he ought to get away for a week and suggested Morecambe. At last he reluctantly agreed and a relief postman took over his round.

The following week he was back on the job. One of his friends said: "By, Tom lad, you look better for your week off; did you go to Morecambe?"

"Nay," replied Tom, "it were such a grand week I've been going round wi' t'other postman."

C H Wood

A doctor arrived at a remote farm in the Moors just in time to deliver the first child of the farmer and his wife. The farmer's face expressed his delight in the birth of a fine baby boy.

The doctor requested the farmer to bring the oil lamp nearer to the bedside - in time to deliver a second child. The farmer's face showed some surprise and anxiety over this state of affairs.

When the doctor requested the farmer to bring the oil lamp nearer, the farmer stood his ground and said firmly: "Nay, doctor, it's t'leet that attracts 'em and this farm only meks enough for two bairns."

Ian P Sampson

An elderly lady who by her mode of dress and her manners looked as if she had suddenly stepped out of a Dickens novel came into the bookshop and nervously asked if there were any blue books for sale. The bookseller was affronted at such a suggestion and gave the old lady a lecture on the damage these books do, especially to the younger generation, finally telling her that he would never allow such questionable books into his shop.

"Oh, I am sorry," said the old lady. "I never realised they would do so much harm, I did not want them to read. I thought a shelf full of good books with blue covers on would tone with my new curtains".

T C (Kit) Calvert

I was watching Old Tom ringing porkers through the snout. Their loud squealings made talking difficult. Tom paused for a moment, the pincers holding the open ring poised ready for the protesting piglet in his lap, and said in all seriousness: "Ah'm fair capped how wimmin can 'bide these 'ere rings through their lugs!"

Norman Ellison

The last time I painted in Dent, a shower of rain induced me to take refuge in a large opening next to a public house. As I was completing the painting, up came a village elder, who looked at the work, then said: "By gum, lad, that's all reight! I'll tell thee what; when tha's done it tha wants to tak it into pub, tha'll gat a fiver for it. I've sin 'em give a fiver for a lot worse na that!"

Percy Monkman

When I was a student at foresters' training school, visits were made by a very eminent entomologist from Oxford University. To assist him with his instruction he would bring into the class-room a large suitcase containing hundreds of boot polish tins. In each tin, carefully mounted and numbered, was a forest insect.

The tins were passed round the class and attempts were made by the students to identify them. Two insects became decapitated, and the head of one insect was carefully attached to the thorax of another and duly presented to the tutor for

"I'm only washing the white ones."

identification. After careful examination, during which the distinguished entomologist went to the window for more light to aid his lens, he pronounced: "This, my boy, is a Humbug!"

Richard Bell

A man entered an inn after closing time and demanded a drink. Upon being refused, he pointed to the wall clock and said: "Yon clock's fast on t'wall," Quick as a flash came the reply from the landlady: "If it worn't fast it 'ud fall on t'floor."

W H Marsden

An accountant was assisting a not-so-young Dales farmer with the work of filling in the application form for registration as a business for VAT. He read out the questions, and the farmer client provided the answers.

Eventually he came to that classic question, which must have been designed especially for Dales businesses: "Will your record be kept on a computer?"

The farmer replied: "My records'll be kept on t'same bl...dy spike they've allus bin kept on!"

R A Stockdale

"He just doesn't care any more, doesn't Harry."

Dick kept a grocery shop in the Dales village and knew how to live and let live. When a business was slack, he would bat, bowl or field on the green with the local youngsters, who loved him. On early closing days, he went fishing with ancient tackle and incredible skill.

One day he abandoned his shop to visit another shop across the green. It had a haberdashery department. Other people were there and Dick enjoyed the social occasion while waiting his turn.

Suddenly he exclaimed: "Dammit, that's a customer going into my shop." The conversation paused, sympathetically. Dick did not stir. A minute, two minutes passed, and he sighed with relief. "It's all reet," he said, "she's comin' out agin."

Brian Belshaw

A villager asked about the proficiency of the local joiner, as he wished to buy a wheelbarrow. "Aye," said a local, "thee go and ask so-and-so to do t'job and if thy wheelbarrow runs as well as 'is water-butts, it'll be a good 'un."

John Schofield

A long-established resident of a Dales village watched with interest the progress of another local resident who became first a Parish Councillor and later a County Councillor. The old 'un was heard to remark: "Well now, unless Bill is careful, he mun find that today's roosters be tomorrow's feather dusters."

Geoffrey G Watson

A Dales farmer had to undergo a rather serious operation which was performed by an eminent Leeds surgeon. In due course the question of paying the bill arose.

"How much dosta want?" the farmer asked.

"Fifty guineas," the surgeon replied.

The farmer proceeded to count the notes very slowly.

"Oh, please," said the surgeon, "give me a cheque and save yourself a lot of trouble."

"Nay, nay," said the farmer, "Ah've put thee down in my income tax as ten tons o' muck."

Kenneth J Bonser

An old and somewhat short-tempered farmer was having great difficulty in getting his sheepdog to drive the flock to another field. In desperation and truly vexed he shouted: "Thoo useless b.... coom 'ere an 'old geeat oppen, an ah'll drive 'em through mesen."

Irene Megginson

A party of ramblers, knowing nothing of the district, was examining the amazing collection of Norber boulders above Crummackdale near Austwick. A knowing local lad appeared and described vividly how, in an Ice Age, the great rocks had been brought from afar by a glacier to their present position.

As he concluded his stirring account, one of the ramblers said: "What happened to the glacier?" The knowing lad paused only for an instant. "Happen it went back for more rocks," he replied.

Ken Willson

Fifty years ago, the Esk Valley was flooded. A man was watching the torrent smash Sleights Bridge. As he stood gawping into the place where the bridge had been, he said: "Deng it, ah's on t'wrang sahde."

Harold Brown

A native of Austwick near Hornsea was known as Long Tom because of his giant size. Times were hard and his cottage roof was leaking but he could not afford the repairs.

He knew where there was a barrel of tar in the barn of one of the locals and on a dark night he waited until well after midnight then, with a bucket on his arm, he trod stealthily through the night to the barn.

Filling his bucket from the tap, he managed to make his way home unobserved and he hid the bucket in the outhouse.

Next morning, he came face to face with the local constable. Tom, astute and cunning though he was, was completely nonplussed by the accusation of theft. "If tha wants to go pinchin' tar, Tom lad," said the policeman, "mek sure tha essent got an hole in thie bucket." Tom looked past the policeman and saw black tar leading from his shed, down the path to the gate and, no doubt, right through the village.

Leslie Simpson

Father had reached the age of 84 years and was not too well. He often remarked it was about time to go, as he was the last of the "old 'uns".

"What about Mr Brown?" asked his son. "He is older than you so why do you worry?"

"Oh, he isn't one of us, he hasn't been in the village long enough yet," replied father.

Mr Brown at that time had been living in the village for nearly 60 years.

E A Wright

On a warm summer evening, a rambler entered a Dales country inn, bought a pint and took a seat in the snug, which was occupied by three grey-bearded dalesmen. After ten minutes' silence, the rambler suggested that the weather was kind. A further ten minutes silent cogitation was broken by: "Aye, but ah reckon it'll rain tomorrow", from one of the dalesmen.

Ruminating on this bold prophecy for ten more minutes, the second dalesman peered through the window and announced: "Nay, ah reckon it'll keep up."

The third dalesman, after a similar time-lapse, emptied his glass, rose to his feet and announced: "Ah'm bahn. Can't stand all this 'ere argyfying."

Arthur Gemmell

A farmer one night saw a light moving across the farmyard. He found on investigation that it was carried by his hired man, who was dressed up and carried a lantern. On being asked where he was going with the lantern, the man replied: "Ah'm off courtin".

"Courtin'?" queried the farmer, "Ah nivver took a lantern when ah went courtin'."

"Naw," said the man, "Ah thowt not when Ah saw thi missus."

Ted Blanchard

Jammy and his school friends were carrying on a vendetta against the local milkman. One day, seeing the milkman along the street, Jammy called out: "Mr Sutcliffe, Mr Sutcliffe, Ah seed 'ee. Ah seed 'ee puttin' watter in t'milk."

Mr Sutcliffe went straight to the schoolmaster and Jammy was duly ticked off and made to promise never to say that again.

A day or so later, when the milkman came along the street, Jammy called out from the street corner: "Mr Sutcliffe, Mr Sutcliffe - tha knaws."

Col Philip Turner van Straubenzee

"Hey, Mam! Can camper have a bucket o' watter?

A young lad turned up at a farm and asked for work. "Hes ta getten onny testimonials?" asked the farmer. "Nay," replied the lad. "Well, tha'd better come back when tha's gotten some." Off went the lad and returned a few days later. "Now me lad, hesta gotten them testimonials?" asked the farmer. "Aye," replied the lad, "I 'ave an' all. I've gotten thine and I'm not comin'."

G Graham Kennewell

A keen ornithologist noticed a bird going into a hole at the side of a tin shack belonging to the petrol station, and he said to his young daughter, who was by this time taking an interest in ornithology: "Now, what kind of bird is that?" She thought for a while, unsuccessfully. He replied: "It's a house sparrow." The child's bright eyes sparkled as she turned and laughed. "It looks more like a garage sparrow to me," she observed.

Bill Sanderson

Sid and Margaret were returning to the city outskirts from a walk. At a very inadequate field gate, some very determined steers were nosing their way into the roadway. Fearing chaos in the gathering gloom, Margaret gallantly offered to hang on to the swaying gate while Sid hurried by a devious route to the farm.

The farmer flung a length of rope and cried out: "'Ere thou art lad, tie yon gate up fer us, will ta?" He promptly shut the door. Sid and Margaret were left musing on the astute economics of some countrymen.

Sid Nicholson

Johnny returned from his school outing to Haworth, "capital" of the Brontë country. With enthusiasm he told his father of all he had seen - the Worth Valley Railway, the Brontë Waterfall, The Brontë Parsonage Museum, the many Brontë teashops, bookshops and souvenir shops. Lastly, he said he had been to Haworth Zoo. "And what did tha' see there?" asked his dad. "A Brontësaurus," said Johnny.

Derek G Widdicombe

A Londoner was watching a local blacksmith making a wrought iron gate. The Londoner said: "It's nice to see a true craftsman at work. I work in the small instrument field where I've got to be accurate to 1/10,000th of an inch.

The blacksmith looked at him and said: "Weel, in that case, thoo'd better stay and watch. Ah's exact."

Peter N Walker

THE DAILY ROUND

LONGSTAFF

A southerner, on holiday in Yorkshire, often frequented the village inn. Here his curiosity was aroused by a three foot six inch man with a cauliflower ear and an insatiable thirst for local ale.

On the last day of his holiday, the visitor made inquiries into the background of this local character. "That man used to be six feet tall," explained the landlord. "His unselfish heroism saved 80 men in a mine accident. He managed to hold up the roof with his head while his mates scrambled out."

"But how did he get his cauliflower ear?" asked the tourist.

"Well, said the landlord, "we had the devil of a job knocking him into place with a shovel!"

Mike Donald

I paid a visit to a barber on market day in a North Riding town recently. As I sat in the chair being shaved I asked the barber how much he charged for shaving.

"Ninepence," he told me.

"That's cheap enough," I commented.

Unfortunately at that moment he accidentally knicked me with the razor, and with profuse apologies dabbed at it with cotton wool.

A bearded old Dalesman who had been waiting with several others called out: "Cheap enough, aye. Ah reckon it's cut price."

TW

I once had a spell of door-to-door salesmanship and in my first inexperienced days I called at one house where a small boy opened the door to my knock.

"Is there no one else in?" I asked.

"Yes, my sister," said the boy brightly.

"Perhaps I could see her," I said.

He disappeared and did not return for several minutes. Then I heard his voice calling: "You'd better come in, I can't lift her out of the playpen."

F Beecroft

Our village butcher, a friendly soul, was gossipy to the point of loquacity to any housewife in a hurry.

One morning a busy lady customer poked her head around the shop door and shouted: "A pound o' steak, Jimmy, an' ah'll call for t'pedigree in't mornin'."

PMB

Overheard in a Driffield shop:

Wolds-type gentleman customer: "Thi crabs is dear. Ah can gerrem at arf that price at t'uther shop."

Fishmonger: "Why don't you gerrem there then?"

Customer: "Cos they eh non."

A G Cammosh

I went into the village store as the shopkeeper and an old farmer were discussing the big race.

"So yer picked a slow 'un, eh?" the shopkeeper asked.

"Well, ah wouldn't say he was slow," the farmer said, "but t'jockey took a packed lunch."

Mary E S Lister

Some years ago I was having a snack in the refreshment room at the old Midland station at Leeds. Near me was a middle aged woman struggling with a hot cup of coffee, trying to gulp it down before train time and keeping an eye on the clock as she did so.

An old farmer near me saw her plight and called out, "Here, missus, tak my cup o' coffee. It's already saucered and blowed".

K Fisher

An old chap from these parts had been off-colour for many months and eventually went to see the doctor.

"What you need is a change of climate," said the doctor.

"Nay," said the ailing man, "Ah've nivver had owt else, living i' Leyburn all mi life."

HH

An advertising campaign for butter was launched in a Bradford suburb.

A little old lady, answering a loud knock on her cottage door, was confronted by a huge, heavily bearded Viking who demanded: "Do you eat Danish butter?"

She replied in a very shaky voice. "No, but a'm bahn to from now on!"

D Hainsworth

A big crowd had gathered round a man in a Yorkshire market place who was selling tins of corn cure. After a long discourse on its qualities he asked if anyone in the crowd had bought a tin from him the week before.

From the back of the crowd came a voice: "Yes, I did."

"And did it do all I said?" asked the salesman.

"Aye, rather. My missus used it to polish t'furniture, and it took all t'nobs off t'chest o' drawers."

F Burley

In a Hawes café one day a farmer's wife told her friend that her husband had just stopped smoking.

"My goodness, that takes some willpower, I think," said her friend.

"Indeed it does," agreed the wife, "and that'd be just what I've got."

John Dickson

The foreman asked a limping man what had happened: "Hurt yourself, Fred?"

Fred: "Nay, I've gotten a nail sticking up in mi' boot."

Foreman: "Then why don't you take it out?"

Fred: "What, in mi' dinner hour?"

SM

Whenever a customer made for the door — having forgotten to pay — a Pickering barber asked him if he had collected his change. One day a farmer from the moors had his hair cut. Then he put his cap and, without paying, strode quickly to the door, pulling it open with a quick jerk.

The barber hurriedly asked him if he had collected his change. The farmer, without a trace of emotion replied: "Nay, I thowt it would do for a tip."

And with that he slammed the door and was gone.

Bert Frank

Some time ago I was introduced to a Lancashire lad. As he took my hand he said: "Tha's from Yorkshire, eh?"

"Aye, lad," I replied.

"'Ere," he said, "give us t'other hand as well. Last Yorkshireman ah shook hands with picked me pocket."

A H Kilburn

The boss caught two workmen sneaking off from the job. "Hey, you!" he called. "Why aren't you working?"

"We are," replied one, "We're carrying this plank to the sawmill."

"Plank?" snapped the boss, "I don't see any plank."

"Well, what d'you know about that, Bill!" cried the workman to his partner. "We've gone and forgot the plank!"

TN

Tom, entering the mill mess room, was greeted with: "Noo, lad, 'ow's tha getting on?"

"Oh, nut sa bad, lad, but I's a lartle bit tired."

"That isn't wi wark, 'cos thu disn't like it all that mitch, does tha?"

"Nay, mebe nut, lad. But thoo naws, a cat likes milk, but thoo nivver knew yan droon itsen amang it, did ta?"

H W Dean

A very large dalesman who visited Leeds was much astonished by the city sights. As he stood gazing at a most imposing building a city man, hurrying past, almost fell over his feet.

"Why don't you keep your big feet out of my way, you great lout?" exclaimed the hasty citizen.

The dalesman, looking down from his superior height, replied slowly: "Thou's noan sa sharp thisell, lad, 'er thou'd a seen 'em, an' kep out ov mi road."

Florence Foster Brook

While visiting his son in London a Dales farmer noticed four road labourers taking a breather, leaning on their shovels.

"Typical southerners," he growled. "Three doin nowt an' one helpin' 'em."

T M Kearns

A spinster, having been listening with delight to the Salvation Army Band outside Morley Town Hall, put a pound note in the hat that was taken round.

The bandmaster thanked her profusely and said: "Hallelujah, that's reight good on yer, missus. Yer can choose onny hymns yer want. What'll it be?"

"I'll hev 'im what plays big drum," was the unexpected reply.

Ken Lemmon

CHURCH AND CHAPEL

Two churchwardens were touring the outlying farms of the parish when they met two Dales farmers who were leaning on a gate. One of the farmers asked a warden: "What's t'after?"

"We're collecting for the church."

"Ah've nowt fer thee," came the reply.

As they turned to go, the farmer called after them: "What's it for, anyhow?"

"A going away present for the vicar," they answered.

"Come 'ere," he said, "Ah'll gi thee summat."

William Ruck

A Yorkshire moorland parson, visiting his flock, called upon an old farmer who rarely went to church.

He was gratified to find him poring intently over his bible, while three pups gambolled at his feet.

"Well, well, John," said the minister. "It is indeed a pleasure to see you improving your old age."

Nowt o' t'sooart," was the reply, "To tell yer t'truth. Ah'm lookin' for names for t'dogs."

E Radcliffe

A group of chapellers called a meeting to discuss the state of the roof. The wealthiest man among them, knowing that he would be expected to fork out much of the estimated £200, insisted that it was not in need of repair.

A large piece of plaster detached itself and hit him squarely on the head.

"Well 'appen it wants repairin'," he conceded. "I'll give you £100."

The minister looked solemnly at the hole in the ceiling and said: "Go on, Lord - hit him again!"

S Cheesbrough

A small boy was taken to his first harvest festival. Among the offerings of fruit and flowers, the bunches of beautiful purple grapes round the pulpit took his fancy.

When the offertory box came round he put in sixpence and said confidently, "Grapes, please."

FM

The weather was very cold, and the organist of a small Yorkshire church reprimanded the caretaker (who was also the organ blower) for not having the church sufficiently heated. "It's almost too cold for me to play the organ," he grumbled.

After the service, the organ blower was heard laughing and said, "He's allus hevving a go at me, but I got me revenge toneet. When he were playing Christians Awake, I were blowing for God Rest Ye Merry Gentlemen."

Dennis Hirst

In a Yorkshire town a series of revival meetings was being held and caused quite a stir. More and more people flocked to the banner.

In this town lived two brothers, in business as coal dealers, and their reputation for honest dealing was not of the highest.

One of the brothers attended the meetings, became "convert-ed" and then set about to reform his kith and kin. In the end it came to a showdown.

The other brother, quite exasperated, retorted thus: "Nah, look here. It's all vary well for thee to talk, but ahm baan to ask thi a straight question: "If ah get converted who does ta think's baan to weigh t'coal?"

H Mallinson

A local preacher, on the first Sunday after the declaration of war in 1939, prayed earnestly:

"Oh Lord, as Thou wilt 'ave seen i' yesterday's Yorkshire Post, them Germans is at it agen."

M Scott

The old farmer at the chapel prayer meeting may have been a bit mixed in his metaphors, but his meaning was in no doubt when he prayed:

"Lord, Lord, if there's a spark of the Divine in us, watter it."

PR

"Poor little tree! Why doesn't someone turn it loose?"

TOWN AND CITY

Blue Scars, badges of honour in mining, are frequently to be seen in the pithead baths of the county, but one that appeared on the bald head of a miner called for special attention. He was asked if he had been struck by a piece of falling coal or bumped by a steel bar.

"Nay," said the miner. "Wife was frying bacon; it burnt and she hit our young 'un. I told her that if she hit him again, I'd hit her. So she hit him, I hit her, and she hit me — wi' t'frying pan!"

Samuel Cheesbrough

The managing director of an old and well-established Bradford business went to see a portrait painter. "My father was the founder of our business and we would like you to paint his portrait, which will be hung in our boardroom," he said.

The painter agreed to accept the commission. "Can we make some arrangements for sittings?" he said.

"I'm afraid that won't be possible. Father's been dead these last ten years or so."

"In that case you probably have photographs from which I can work?"

"Unfortunately, no. Father was a very shy and retiring man and was never photographed. But..." (here the managing director drew from his pocket a foolscap sheet of paper) "... I have written a full detailed description of him, shape of head, shape of nose and mouth, colour of hair and eyes and so on, from which I'm sure you can work."

The artist was sceptical but agreed to continue with the commission. Three months later the managing director was invited to the studio of the artist who, upon unveiling the finished portrait, asked: "What do you think of that?"

After a lengthy pause came the reply. "Marvellous! Absolutely marvellous! That's the old man all right ... but by golly! How he's changed!"

Ionicus

As a speaker of the Royal Society of St George, I love to think of St George as a Yorkshireman who remarked, while waiting for battle in the arena of Rome: "I've a reight interesting tale ti tell thee, Joe, but we'll ha' to wait till we've finished this job, for see they're lettin' lions in."

Bill Hebden

Joe was an artisan at a big Leeds engineering works in the early 1900s, when the London and North Western Railway started cheap day trips to the North Wales coast. Joe went on one.

Next morning he arrived at work, hung up his cap and went to his lathe. Up comes the foreman: "Naa Joe, where was ta yesterday? Badly?"

"No, gaffer, there were a cheap trip to Bangor, so I went on it."

"Oh, tha' did, didst tha — well, Joe lad, tha can get thi cap an' go to Bangor agean."

John Keave

An "off-comed un" arrived in Silsden and asked a bystander the way to Willie Inman's house. Taking him by the arm and emphasising his directions with expansive gestures, the bystander said: "Go up theer, an' turn ower John Berry brig, an' then goa past Joan o'Will's, past Sammy Shoemaker's, on bi Tom o'Bill's, through t'Bell Square, past owd Dick Wood's, ower t'street brig, then turn up at Cat Hoil end, goa past Henry o'Joss's an' tha's almost theer — he lives anent Nan o'Simon's."

John Waddington Feather

A wonderful company of senior citizens called "The Evergreens" was performing its usual two hour show. After about 40 minutes, the curtain came down for a scene change. Five minutes passed and there was still no cue from back-stage to commence the next scene. By this time the pianist had

"Ploughman's lunch, please"

exhausted practically all her "incidental" music.

Frantically, I tore back-stage to get things moving again. To my horror I found no one there. Rushing upstairs to the dressing rooms, I saw the dear old ladies, all 25 of them, standing around drinking tea and eating sandwiches. "What in the world do you think you're doing?" I demanded, almost lost for words. "Weel," said a young sprightly 70 year old, "Charlie and 'is missus arrived wi' tea an' we thowt we'd sup it while it were 'ot."

Denis Cooper

A country man got a job in the city. For the first few nights he had little sleep for he was not used to city lights shining all night through his uncurtained window. He blacked out the window with paint.

The next night he slept so soundly that he was late for work. The foreman was so furious that he had to remonstrate: "Ah'm nobbut half an arh late."

Said the foreman: "And where wor ta yusterday and t'day afooar?"

George Taylor

After a coronation, the King and Queen left Westminster Abbey. The thrones were corded off, but a Gold Staff officer found a Yorkshire mayor had slipped under, had sat on the King's throne and was now getting out.

Gold Stick cried: "My friend, you must not go in there." His worship came steadily up, ruddy-faced and smiling and said "Young man, tha' art too late — ah've just done it."

Frank Hale

After the 1939-45 war, the government gave some "jobs for the boys", including bowler-hatted military men, in the nationalised industries. Coal mining was one of them. This caused good deal of heart-burning among practical mine managers.

At a meeting, a former military man asked: "What's wrong with the coal industry?" Upon which the gaunt figure of a veteran manager rose slowly from a chair. Pointing a bony finger at the platform, he uttered one word: "Thee!"

W R Lane

When the Slubthorpe Amateur Operatic Society was putting on a production of "Good Night Vienna", the small but ambitious and not altogether untalented company — reinforced for the occasion by press ganged school children, husbands, sisters, Young Farmers and a couple of au pair girls — had fought its way through the final dress rehearsal.

George, the caretaker of the hall in which the production was to be staged, had watched the last 45 minutes of a battle which should have ended an hour an a half previously. It would be all right on the night.

The members of the cast assembled on stage for a verdict, anticipatory of his accolade. "Now then, George, how do you think "Good Night Vienna" will do for Slubthorpe?" A moment of feigned deliberation. "Reckon abaht as well as "Good Night Slubthorpe" 'ud do for Vienna."

Howard Strick

Two married women worked next to each other in a woollen mill in Dewsbury but were fed up with their jobs and wanted to leave. One Friday, one of them collected her insurance card and told her friend that she had finished.

"How did you get your husband to agree?" asked the other.

"It wer easy", replied her friend. "I just told him that t'foreman were making eyes at me and he told me I had to leave straight away."

"By gum," was the reply, "I'll have a go at that."

The same night she told her husband that the foreman kept winking at her.

"Ee," he replied. "That's a good sign. Wink back at him a few times and mebbe you'll get another couple o' looms."

John Harold Clucas

FAMILY MATTERS

Two men met in the market place at Ripon one Thursday Jack was surprised to see Bill, who had recently married, looking very troubled.

"What's up wi' thi?" said Jack. "Are ta stalled o' wedded life bi nah?"

"Ah am," said Bill, "Ah'm sick on it. At's allus naggin, abah brass, morn, nooin, an' neet. Ivvery time t'wife sees me, it' brass, brass, brass."

"That must be awkward for thee. What does soo do wi' it thinks ta?" said Jack.

"Nay, Ah'll goa to hummer of Ah knaw. Ah heven't gi'en he onny yet."

E Tyso

I remember on my marriage an old Yorkshireman saying t me: "Congratulations, lad. Tha's at'end o' thi troubles now."

"Thank you," I replied. "That's nice to know."

"Aye," he said, "t'forend!"

A L Braithwait

"Harry always comes home dog tired these days."

When dances crowded fast upon each other in Dales villages, every local institution had its own dance to raise money. The participants were not only the members of the younger generation but parents and grandparents, too. Hence the following story:

Father had returned home early from the dance — at midnight. His daughter came in about 1.00am. Mother returned a few minutes later and was about to lock up when the daughter called out: "Don't lock the door, mother — grandma isn't i' yet!"

AKT

In the days before radio and television, when even the buying of a newspaper was considered to be something of an indulgence, the people of the north-eastern dales would often turn to their doctor for "t'latest".

On one such occasion, during the 1914-18 war, a patient asked about the movement of the enemy.

"Well," replied the doctor, "my paper says they were on the run yesterday, and we've driven them right back."

"Driven 'em?" exclaimed the patient contemptuously. "By! Ah'd ha' made 'em walk, howiver!"

Brenda H English

Ben was a minder in a Bradford mill and was well-known for his parsimonious habits, never having been known to have a day off work.

One afternoon his workmates noticed him looking frequently out of the window. When asked the reason Ben replied: "Nay, Ah war only watchin' for t'funeral. They're buryin' t'wife today, tha knows."

Alice Kelsall

We were chatting with friends one evening when one of our male companions remarked that some of his friends were hen-pecked.

My husband promptly replied: "Eh, bur it's grand bein' pecked wi' t'reight 'en."

Jane Carroll

Two elderly dalesmen in Leyburn market place were discussing the serious ailment of a third.

"Aye," said one, "ah reckon only a post-mortem will show what it is."

"Maybe," replied the other. "But he's so weak he'd never stand that."

W S Parks

A young couple in Harrogate did very well in their married life until the wife became enthusiastic about a cookery book on how to use up leftovers. Although the husband always asked a blessing before each meal, one day he merely lifted the lid of the dish and then replaced it.

"Why don't you ask a blessing?" asked his wife.

"I reckon everything in that dish has already been blessed six times," he replied.

H Lodge

A North Yorkshire doctor called at a cottage to inquire about his patient. "Did your husband take his medicine religiously, as I told him?" he asked.

"Nay, I'm afraid not, doctor; he swore every time I gave him a dose."

K Marsden

Joe and his wife, after an even hotter row than usual, sat sulking, he on one side of the fire, she on the other, with the cat on the rug between them.

When it seemed that the sullen silence would never be broken Joe slowly uncrossed, then recrossed his legs, sighed and said "Ee, Ah wish one of us three were deead. An, Ah dooan't meean missen."

Just then the cat looked and mewed. "Ah dooan't meean thee nawther!" said Joe.

James R Gregson

While serving at my stall in Doncaster market I could not help hearing two middle-aged ladies in conversation. They were apparently discussing a third lady who did not find favour with them.

"'ere! Charles! Knock the alarm off will you dear!"

Said one lady to the other: "Ee, she's as miserable as sin! Niver speaks to anybody, and when she does she says nawt."

B Ebb

Owd Sam knew nowt abaht gardening, but thowt he'd plant some taties. As he was gathering t'crop, Josh — his next door neighbour — ast him how he'd done.

"Well," said Owd Sam, "just so-so. Ah've gotten some as big as peas and some as big as marbles, but Ah've hed a hell of a lot of little 'uns an' all!"

T A Rogers

Did you hear that owd Dick Horsfall's gettin' wed again?" said Sam in the local.

"You'd have thought he were owd enough to know better nor that."

"Aye, he does know better, lad," said Bill. "But trouble is, he met a widder who knew better still!"

J E Sparke

One teatime a friend was unsuccessfully trying to coax her small son to eat some prunes. "God'll punish yer if yer dooan't eit 'em," she said, but the little lad still refused.

"Reeight," said mother, "yer goin' straight to bed." She undressed the lad and put him to bed.

During the evening there was a terrific thunderstorm and mother thought the lad would be scared; she went upstairs. He was pacing about in front of the window muttering: "Thunder, leetnin', 'Es makkin a hek of a fuss ovver a few prunes!"

H Hellewell

Heard at a WI meeting: "And how is your husband getting on?"

"I hardly know. He is so busy I only see him for about an hour a day."

"Oh, you poor thing. I am sorry."

"Oh, that's all right. The hour soon passes."

MW

"Funny how you never see any animals on these nature trails."

A friend whose fair hair was darkening a little decided that a special shampoo was called for. The next day, her locks became a few shades lighter.

During the evening meal her teenage son kept giving her puzzling looks. After a while he said: "Have you been washing your hair, mum?"

"Yes," she replied.

Silence for a while, but the puzzled looks continued, then came the outburst: "By gum, it must er bin mucky."

N Barley

Coming from Rosedale to Darlington at the age of five I was asked by the schoolmaster if I knew where I was born.

I said: "Aye, in't back bedroom."

Phyllis Howitt

An East Riding man, troubled by his wife's reckless way with money, finally gave her an account book and £20 for housekeeping.

"Now," he said, "Thoo put down what Ah've gi'en thoo on one page, and on t'opposite page put down what thoo's done wi' it. Then thoo'll know wheer all t'money's gone."

At the end of the week she presented the book eagerly to her husband. "Look, I've done just as you told me."

And she had. On one page was written: "Received £20." On the opposite page was written: "Spent it all."

E Watson

My mother, who is aged 86, was one of a large family, and anything which was not eaten appeared on the table at the next mealtime. Her youngest brother was a very stubborn little boy and often refused his food.

On one occasion, he refused to eat his gruel, and my grandmother must have reached the end of her patience, for she said: "Well, it's awther in thi or on thi," and promptly emptied the contents of the bowl over his head!

B Downie

Old George had trouble with his leg. He went to the surgery about it. As he wrote out a prescription, the doctor said: "Let me see, George, how old are you?"

"Eighty-fower," replied George.

"Well, now," said the doctor: "I think, don't you, that we can put this bad leg of yours down to old age?"

"Nowt o' t'sort," said George, indignantly. "T'other leg's same age an' there's nowt wrong wi' that."

RR

A neighbour, calling on a friend, found him scraping wallpaper off the walls.

He asked: "Are you decorating, George?"

George, with a hurt look: "No, we're removing."

Arnold Witcomb

My word, you must have cost your mother a mint of money," said a lady to two youngsters at Redcar who had been filling themselves with ice-cream, peanuts and lollipops all afternoon.

"No, we 'aven't," retorted the little girl. "She gorrus on the National Health."

J E Sparke

When in the Grosmont-Egton district, a driver stopped her car on a steep hill to ask an old lady at her garden gate: "Is this hill dangerous?"

"Not here it isn't," was the reply, "it's doon at t'bottom where they all kills thersens."

Florence Hopper

My cousin was looking for somewhere to camp above Hunmanby, near Scarborough. A promising pitch was a nearby field and, seeing two small boys, he inquired whose field it was.

"Yon's Mosey's field," said the elder.

The little boy, aged about five, added dreamily: "Mosey's was the feller in t'Bible who saw t'bonnin bush, and God said, 'Moses, tek yer beeuts off — yon's Holy Ground where yer stannin'.'"

E M Salisbury

AT THE FARM

A farmer had been trying unsuccessfully for half an hour to get two mules into a horse box. The village parson came up the lane just when the farmer's patience was exhausted.

"Now, Sam. You look fairly bothered. What's the matter?" he asked.

"Thou art just t'chap I wanted to see, parson," replied Sam. "Can ta tell me how Noah managed to get two o' these devils into t'ark?"

T H Watson

Two Methodist local preachers were being entertained to dinner by a local farmer. The farmer's wife had done them proud with two of their own reared chickens.

During the dinner, the farmer received an emergency call to his stock and when he returned the visitors had eaten so heartily that they had cleared the lot and he had to make do with corned beef.

He felt a bit disgruntled, but after the meal took them round his poultry enterprise. The two men praised the excellence of his stock, especially his male bird.

"Aye," said the farmer, thinking of his corned beef dinner, "he ought to feel proud of hissen; he has two sons in t'ministry!"

W Stockdale

Intelligence was not his strong point, but he did manage to keep his job on a Yorkshire farm.

One day the farmer sent him for a turnip, and in reply to the question "What size?" said: "Oh, as big as your head, you fool."

Some two hours later a friend called at the farm and said to the farmer: "What's the matter with your odd job man?"

"Why?" asked the farmer, "what's he doing?"

"Well, I don't quite know," replied the friend, "but when I came along the path, I saw him sitting in one of your fields pulling up turnips as fast as he could and trying his cap on them."

E Radcliffe

One day, Fred was in a field with the farmer manuring potato rows prior to the potatoes being set.

"Put plenty on, me lad," said the farmer, "taties are hungry things."

"So Ah noaticed at dinner time," said Fred, "in the meeat and tatie pie we had for dinner. Why, taties in t'bit Ah got had eaten all t'meeat up."

J T Harrison

When an old Wolds farmer was told by his doctor to have a simpler diet, he objected strongly.

"Aw'm nut gooing to starve mysen to death for t'sake o' living a few years longer."

T Caldwell

Up in Swaledale some years ago there lived an old chap who went round doing odd jobs for which he was rewarded by small sums of money or something off the farm.

One December he reminded one farmer: "Ah thowt ye said ye were goin' to gie me a turkey for Christmas."

"Aye," said the farmer. "Appen Ah did. But it got better."

KI

A Yorkshire horse deal was never a very speedy operation, and often several hours elapsed before the money and the horse changed hands.

One man sold a horse with the comment: "I'm afraid it doesn't look so good."

"Looks all reight to me," said the buyer.

But the buyer was back a few hours later. "That hoss you selled me's blind i' one eye," he declared.

"Aye," said the dealer, "I telled thee it didn't look soa good!"

M Roberts

After working alongside his men all one Monday, a Yorkshire farmer did not seem happy with the results of the day's labour.

Turning to them, he said: "Just think on. A day and an arf after tomorrer the biggest arf o' the week will a gone, an' nowt done."

Ken Gill

Seen written in the grime on a particularly dirty Land Rover in the local market: "Don't wash me: plant summat."

M Rosamund

They had given a Wharfedale farmer a barometer to mark his silver wedding, and some days later he met an old crony who asked him if he liked his present.

"Nay," he said. "Ah think nowt to it. You can't depend on it. One day it says one thing and t'next it says summat different."

E Pearson

A farmer at Clayton Heights asked his son to fetch one of the two horses from the field and harness it to the trap to take him to Barnsley.

"Which horse shall I fetch, dad?" asked the boy.

"Bring t'oldest, lad," said his father. "We'll use t'oldest up first."

"If it's a case o' that, dad," replied the boy, "I think tha'd better go for it."

J W Hinchcliff

Charlie was desperate for work and had been practically all round Cawood without any success. The last straw came when he asked at a farm for a job making hay, only to be told by the farmer: "The sun makes my hay."

Next spring, labour was scarce and the boot was on the other foot. The same farmer approached Charlie and asked him to strike turnips for him.

"Nay," said Charlie "the sun makes your hay — then let the lightning strike thi turnips."

Two men were returning home to Dent from Sedbergh on a Saturday night after having a few pints of beer. They came to a gate with a notice on it: "This field for sale."

One of them turned to t'other and said: "I would ha' bought that, but I ha' nowhere to put it."

S E Middleton

Some years ago, on a fine June morning, a Yorkshire farmer, who was noted for his meanness, hitched his horse to the mowing machine as low as possible, in order to get a maximum crop.

The field was bumpy and soon the prongs caught in the

"If you haven't got my milk cheque I'm filling it in again."

ground. The shaft broke with a sickening crunch.

"Ah!" said the neighbouring farmer who was looking on, "that's what comes o' trying to plew as well as moo!"

Jack Wilcock

A young man from the city thought he would like a country job for a change and went to call on a farmer.

"Well," said the farmer, "I don't know what a city man could do here. What were you?"

"I was a fitter-mechanic."

"Do you think you could shoe a horse?"

"Well," said the mechanic, "I'm willing to try."

"All right. I've got to go into the village for an hour or so. See what you can make of the job."

When the farmer returned he found the horse lying on its back, with all four feet stuck in the air. It had been shod, though, and the job had been well done.

"You've made a good fist of that," he complimented, "but what's the matter with the horse? He looks a bit odd."

"I've been worrying about that," replied the mechanic. "He's been like that ever since I took him out of the vice."

WE

A farm labourer was leading a horse down a road where two ladies in their car left him insufficient room to pass. He told them so — bluntly.

After a complaint his farmer employer told him to apologise. So in the evening he called upon the ladies. Standing before them, cap in hand, he asked them if they were the two ladies he had told to go to hell when he passed them in the morning.

"Yes, we are," they said.

"Well, I've come to tell yer, yer needn't go."

M A McHugh

A farmer surprised his neighbours by selling an old and battered van and buying a new Rolls Royce.

"And how are you liking your new car?" a friend inquired.

"Fine," replied the farmer.

"What is it about the Rolls that suits you best, then?"

The farmer considered before replying.

"Why now, I'd say it's the glass screen between front and rear... it's nice being able to drive without the coo's licking t'back o' mi neck."

M Benton

A farmhand named John was instructed by his employer to bury a sheep in the far field. "You may as well clip her," said the farmer. "Take those shears and a sack with you."

John arrived back at the farm late for dinner. After a while the farmer said: "Did you manage all right, John?"

"Yes," said John.

"Then where is the wool?" asked the farmer.

"Oh," said John, "I put that in first."

John W Sanderson

**"I don't want a filing cabinet as a Christmas present
... what I want is an incinerator."**

About the turn of the century my grandfather and grandmother had engaged a labourer at Stockton "Hirings" to help on their farm and were taking him with them in their horse and trap.

My grandmother, who "wore the trousers" in the household, was filling in the time usefully to her way of thinking by detailing to the man the various duties he would have to fulfil.

After a quarter of an hour or thereabouts, she paused for breath, whereupon the man turned to my grandfather and enquired: "Hey, mister, hast thoo much clay o' t'farm?"

"Nay, not si much, but mebbe there's a bit by t'beck i' t'Fower Yakker; it's clarty there. Why dost thoo ask, like?"

"Ee, that's a pity," replied the man, "Ah was aimin' ti mak thoo a few bricks i' ma spare tahme!"

CC

A Wolds farmer devised a marvellous scarecrow. It waved its arms in the breeze. It had an alarming tin rattle that went off at intervals. And it carried a dummy gun.

I asked him if it really scared the birds after all his effort.

"Noo, Ah reckon it does. Whya, only the other day they crows brought back some corn they had stole from me two years ago."

HW

Talk (pre-war) in the Buck Inn at Cop Gate was running on the wonders of plastic surgery. Old Fred Garbutt joined in. "Oor vet's as good as onny on 'em", he said ruminatively. "Last harvest, t'lad chanced ti ek a greeat piece oot ov his thigh wi t'reaper.

"He was in a bad way, but t'vet com up tiv a new-cauven coo, an he fettled t'lad as weel - he just took a slice off t'coo's udder an' stitched it on, shairp as owt.

T'lad mended quick, an' noo he's givin' three gallon a milk a day, sucklin' tweea calves, and doin' a day's work inti t'bargain!"

Bill Cowley

HOLIDAY JOYS

A young Yorkshire lady, planning to go on holiday to Scarborough with her girl friend, was bitterly disappointed when, a week or so before the date of departure, her friend cried off.

However, her mother suggested that she put an advertisement in the local paper reading: "Attractive young lady seeks companion for holiday in Scarborough." This she did, under a box number.

Some days later, she was reading through some replies to the advertisement when she burst out laughing. "What's the matter?" asked her mother. "Well," replied the girl, "there's one here from dad!"

David Jenkinson

Jack had been ill for some time but he was making a good recovery and was sent to Scarborough by his doctor for a week's convalescence.

Unfortunately, towards the end of the week he suffered a relapse and suddenly died. His body was taken home to Pudsey and, as the relatives stood around the coffin paying their last respects and consoling his widow, his sister turned to her and said, "Ee, lass, but he's a lovely colour — that week in Scarborough did him a world of good."

Stephen Fewster

The story is told at Whitby of a holidaymaker who thought he would try his novice hand at fishing from the pier.

He spent nearly an hour in patience before he reached up a very fine flat fish, which his fishing companions all envied. Then, suddenly, he threw it back into the sea.

"Why did you do that?" asked a fellow fisherman.

"Well, I don't want one that's been trodden on," said the holidaymaker."

T Kilby

On the first day of our holiday at Whitby we stopped to admire the whale jawbone arch on the West Cliff.

I remarked to my grandmother how large they were. She did

not seem to be very impressed. After a brief silence she replied: "Aye, they'll tell thee owt these days. They can't be real bones — they're exactly t'same size."

David E Stead

An American approached a fisherman on the quayside at Whitby and, pointing up to the West Cliff hotels, he laughed and said: "We are building bigger fish and chip shops in the States."

Next day, the American came to the same fisherman on the quay and, pointing to the two lighthouses on the piers, asked what they were. The answer came back quickly: "They're salt and pepper pots for thy fish and chip shops."

Eric Turner

A visitor in a small fishing village on the East Yorkshire coast was heard to remark to one of the locals: "Whatever do you find to do down here during the winter?"

To which came the blunt reply: "T'same as i' summer, but wi' us overcoats on!"

A E Alba

"Poor George simply CAN'T relax!"

The two men left Bridlington Harbour in perfect weather and went out rather further than usual. They had been fishing for some time with great enjoyment when a sudden squall sprang up.

The wind lashed the sea into great waves, the rain poured down and their small boat looked in danger of capsizing.

In great terror the two old men began to pray aloud: "Oh God, send down thy only son to save us," cried one, but his friend shouted him down. "Nay God, cum down thisell do, t'save is, fer this is noa lad's job."

Florence F Brook

"Son of the soil? No, he's a bank manager staying in his holiday cottage next door!"

A fellow lodger in a London boarding house told me he had just spent a holiday at a Yorkshire moors village. I asked him how he had enjoyed it.

"Oh, it was a terrible place," he said. "I think it was a waste of a 'oliday. You see, you couldn't get anywhere without walking."

D Fletcher

My holiday was cut short when I was called home, leaving my own family behind, due to my father's being taken very ill and rushed into hospital.

Accommodation for my invalid mother was secured in an Old People's Home and for the next two-and-a-half weeks I visited them both every day, fetched and carried and generally ran about to please them, by which time the patients looked fitter than the visitor.

The day came for my father's discharge. I prepared and restocked the house for their return, collected my father's clothes in accordance with his detailed instructions and delivered them to his bedside, leaving him behind the bedside curtains to get dressed.

A moment later I was recalled and, when I inquired if everything was all right, I was told bluntly: "Nay lad, yuv brought t'wrong tie."

K Brown

My mother and my uncle were watching the fishing boats coming in at Filey.

"Had any luck?" my uncle asked one man.

"Haven't had a bite all day," he replied.

After he'd gone my mother said quite seriously: "Poor man, he must be hungry. Why didn't he take some sandwiches with him?"

J Husband

A visitor to Scarborough got into conversation with one of the old fishermen on the West Pier and they were talking generally about Scarborough as a fishing community.

The fisherman went on to say that his family line had been traced back to the year 1200 and that they had always been associated with Scarborough's fishing industry.

The visitor then jokingly remarked: "I suppose if you go back far enough, you will find that one of your ancestors sailed with Noah in the Ark."

To which the fisherman replied: "I don't think so; you see, we've always had our own boat."

Len Dobson

A Minister was having a holiday in a Dales village. Coming down to breakfast on the first morning he could hear the lady of the house singing: "Nearer, my God, to thee."

He remarked how pleasant it was to hear the good old hymn and she replied: "Oh! That's the one I boil the eggs with; one verse for 'oft and two for hard."

Ann Watson

"It says, "Get away from the rat-race with our farmhouse holidays!"

46

MUSICAL MOMENTS

In the '30s my father was secretary of an amateur concert party which used to perform mainly at church socials and the like. One black winter Saturday evening they arrived at a little church where they were to perform in the church hall and were met by the verger.

"Theer's dressin' room," he said, indicating a small vestry.

"Dressing room?" queried my dad, "but there are ladies and gentlemen in the party."

"Well," replied the old man belligerently, "What's matter? 'A' they 'ad words or summat?"

JB

A distinguished conductor was rehearsing a Yorkshire choir in Handel's Messiah. Not liking the women's rendering of "For Unto Us a Child is Born", he rapped sharply for attention and said: "Just a little more reverence, please — and not quite so much astonishment."

PG

"AAAaahh! That's better!"

The occasion was the performance of the annual chapel Messiah and platform space was very limited. John — that lovable giant of a man — revelled in the aria "Thy Trumpet Shall Sound" and he left his hearers in no doubt that "The dead shall be raised incorruptible".

At rehearsal, limbering up, so to say, for his great moment, John raised his long ceremonial trumpet to his lips and thereupon realised that, when extended to playing position, the bell of his instrument would barely miss the ear of the principal cellist. The fortissimo climax would surely blow the said cellist right out of the chapel on to the Yorkshire Moors.

Choosing an appropriate moment, John leaned forward, tapped the endangered player on the shoulder and remarked, "Ah say, George, if ah wer' thee, ah'd shift!"

Arthur Percival

A couple went to a concert at the Albert Hall. The hall was so tightly packed it was very uncomfortable.

"No wonder people don't come here," the wife said. "It's so crowded!"

Betty Bartle

A SPORTING LIFE

Shooting on the Knostrop Range at Leeds, I watched a club-mate put in eight perfect bulls and then two shots wide to the left.

"The wind caught you up there, Norman," I remarked.

"Aye, ruddy thing. It was blowin' t'other way last week," he replied.

(Major) J P Baslington

Cricket was being played on the hillside near Huddersfield and the stumper was batting. Never in his life had he reached the half century and here he was with his score at 49 runs.

He had to face the fast bowler, who with his delivery dropped the ball on a "bare patch". The ball flew up hitting the batter on

"Just how long do we have to wait for the photographer to arrive?"

the top of his head, rising in the air into the hands of the wicketkeeper, who caught it and appealed for a catch.

The umpire slowly and deliberately put up his finger denoting the decision of "Out....caught".

When the stumper had recovered from rubbing his head and saw the umpire's decision he said, "Nay, umpire tha cannot gi' me aht for that 'un. It 'it me on top o' t'hed."

"Aah," said the umpire. "Aah knew it 'it a bit a wood summah. Get thi back to t'tent..."

Bert Ripley

A small boy, newly arrived in a Dales village, asked a local youth if there was any fishing nearby. "Aye lad — there's a pond in t'wood."

The boy said: "Thanks, mister." He rushed off, found the pond, giving but a glance at the sign which, had he been able to read, said: "No fishing."

His concentration on angling was soon shattered when an irate voice roared in his ear: "Carn't tha read what it says on t'sign, lad — it says ner fishin."

Taken aback, but quick as a flash, the boy replied: "Don't thi believe it Mister — I've cop't fur already an' they aren't arf big 'uns."

Edward Hinchcliffe

Two Leeds men were playing golf on the Temple Newsam course. One was a good player, the other a "rabbit" — in many senses.

After a series of fruitless shots the "rabbit" declared sadly, "I'd move heaven and earth to play this game well."

"Nay, keep on trying," said the partner. "Tha's only heaven to move now."

F Harrison

Sam is one of our veteran bowlers and a very good one and a big favourite with the "crowd", but in the game last week, Sam was losing.

Said one of his supporters, "Come on, Sam, buck up, tak' thi coit off."

"Nay, by gum," Sam replied, "Ah nivver took it off when Ah wor werkin', am noon barn to tak it off when am laikin'."

A Robinson

During a Dales cricket match, one of the opening batsmen snicked the ball into the stumper's hands.

Upon appealing, the umpire gave the decision: "Not out!"

In the same over the batsman, an honest fellow whose conscience troubled him, got to the other end and said to the umpire: "Tha knaws ah 'it that ball."

"Ah knaw tha did," responded that worthy, "but it wor nobbut slight."

ER

A well-known Yorkshire master of the hunt, equally renowned for his vocabulary, dealt drastically with a young woman who, coming up behind the rest of the field at a check, signalled her arrival by jumping a gap in a stone wall and landing on top of one of the hounds.

The victim gave a yell which only a hound could produce.

Everyone was silent save the hound, and then above his cries was heard the stentorian voice of the master, couched in terms of sublime sarcasm: "Who owns that woman?"

ER

An enthusiastic angler in a Dales village hooked a monster fish on the first day of the new season. He looked at it and then threw it back into the stream.

"What have you done that for?" he was asked. "It was big enough to take."

"Aye," said the man. "Maybe it was, but if I'd taken that home no one would have believed I'd caught it."

J Briggs

This story illustrates Yorkshire dryness, bullish patriotism ("When you've seen Yorkshire, you've seen England") and grit. I was playing cricket for the local side in an away match at a neighbouring village.

In the first four balls, "their" umpire disallowed two l.b.w. appeals by our opening fast bowler, who is also the captain.

Hitching his trousers for the task ahead, he bellowed out in a voice which could be heard back in our own village: "Right, lads, we'll get nowt here. We'll just have to bowl this lot out."

Harry Mead

At a keenly contested cricket match in South Yorkshire, where feelings ran pretty high and the umpires were of doubtful integrity, a batsman was given out on a very questionable decision of l.b.w.

The unfortunate batsman demonstrated at the wicket that he could not possibly be out and he then walked to the pavilion, protesting on the way.

As the batsman was nearing the pavilion and the commotion had subdued, a wag called out from the crowd: "Thee look in t'paper toneet, tha'll know whether tha'r art or not."

C Matthews

A match took place between traditionally rival teams in Yorkshire. The match had reached a critical stage, with the scores equal and each side trying ferociously to gain an advantage.

Several players had already been carried off and several more had their jerseys ripped when a particularly strong kick by one of the full-backs sent the ball right out of the ground.

The players hesitated, wondering what was to happen next. They were spurred on to further violence by a voice from the crowd: "Never mind t'ball, lads; get on with t'game!"

Lee Vincent

It was the first day of a county match, Yorkshire versus Glamorgan at Harrogate. An old-age pensioner went along to pay his membership subscription and he and the secretary chatted about the good weather.

Said the secretary: "You'd have thought there'd be more people in the ground on a lovely day like this."

The pensioner remarked: "I wouldn't worry; it'll fill up after lunch."

The secretary asked why that was and the pensioner replied: "It's half day at Pateley Bridge."

Fred Trueman

THE INNER MAN

An old farming couple from Calderdale had been shopping in Halifax. They were boarding the one and only bus back to their village when the conductor informed the farmer that there was only room for one person.

Without more ado, the farmer climbed aboard the bus and turning to his wife, who was behind him, said: "I'll have a cup o' tea waiting for thee when tha gets home."

Ian Kendall

A rather flustered new curate of a country church inadvertently misquoted his text by saying, "2,000 loaves and two small fishes fed the five persons." At the end, an old Dales character was clearly heard by all to say that he had thought "nowt o' that" as he could have done it himself.

The following Sunday, to everyone's surprise, the text was the same — but the miracle was correctly quoted, "Two loaves and five small fishes fed the 5,000." At this point the curate leant over the pulpit, looked at the Dales character and said: "Mr Smith, I don't think you could do that now, could you?"

"Oh yes, I could," said Fred Smith.

"How?" asked the curate.

"From the lot left over from last Sunday," said Fred.

John Hepper

After a lengthy walk and with a hearty appetite, a hiker found himself outside a village café with a sign : "Beans, Spam and Chips". The hiker went inside and asked the proprietor, "Have you anything else other than the beans, spam and chips?"

"Oh yes," said the proprietor. "What are they?" asked the hiker. "All sorts," replied the café owner. "We've bacon, spam and chips; mushy peas, spam and chips; sausage, spam and chips, and – and – spam and chips."

Douglas B Smith

The hotel proprietor asked his guest how he would like his breakfast eggs. "I want one so hard you could throw it on the floor and it would bounce, and the other so soft it would fly into my face when I open it," was the reply.

**"Ah'm ready for some dinner, lass.
How's yon new help up from t'city shapin'?"**

"I'm not sure we can manage that," said the proprietor.
"Well, you did it yesterday — it shouldn't be too difficult to repeat the process."

S L Henderson-Smith

A boy and his family moved from Yorkshire to Lancashire. Albert, being naturally taciturn, refused to speak when he attended his new school and a succession of teachers, psychologists, speech therapists and psychiatrists were of no avail.

One day, at school dinner, Albert spoke out, "This Yorkshire puddin's terrible." His teachers were overjoyed, but his headmaster was puzzled. "Why have you not spoken before?" he said.

"Well," said Albert, surprised, "up to now t'Yorkshire puddin's been aw reet."

Frank Pedley

RATHER POORLY

During a grim Yorkshire winter, a Dales joiner could not complete his normal routine because of the snow. He was constructing a coffin in his shop when a friend called.

"Who's that for?" enquired his friend.

"For me," replied the joiner, adding: "I was a bit slack so I thought I would make my own coffin."

"If you're so slack," continued his friend, "you'd better make me one!"

Alan Jones

A parish council clerk announced at a meeting of the Council that the death rate in the Rural District was 6.8. This statement somewhat mystified his chairman, who said he could understand the six deaths but the .8 was not clear to him. The clerk, who always liked to have the last word, having given his chairman a long-suffering look, replied that the position was that six folk had died - and "t'other eight are on t'point of dying."

G C Robinson

An old Yorkshireman was lying in bed approaching the end. His wife and daughter stood at the end of the bed.

Said the daughter to the wife: "I don't think he's long to go now."

The man's squeaky voice was heard from the bed: "Nay, I'm not so bad today."

"Hod thi din," said his wife. "T'doctor knaws better than thee."

Terry Logan

An artist was painting at Bolton Castle when a local farmer stopped to talk and to view the work in progress. They conversed for some time. Then there was a short silence. Said the farmer: "Tell me, is it reight you fellers nivver 'ave owt till ye dee?"

E Charles Simpson

A mayor, who had had a very busy year, became ill. The Council met and it was proposed that an Alderman should go to the Mayor's house and express the sympathy of the members. The Alderman said to the Mayor: "Last night it was proposed that I come round and express the Council's sympathy and the hope that you will soon recover and it was passed — eight votes to seven."

Fred Woodall

"Somebody has cut the appendix out of this book."

"Keep off caviare, asparagus tips and champagne."

A young Yorkshireman with a not-too-serious complaint paid for a private consultation. The specialist arranged for him to attend the hospital for an operation. On reaching the operating theatre, the patient was greeted by the surgeon wearing his mask and gown who asked: "Are you having it done "private" or National Health?" "What's the difference?" asked the young man on the trolley. "Well," replied the surgeon, "if you have it done "private" we sharpen the knives."

Sam Wood

When I first started in practice some 45 years ago, I was living in a village on the outskirts of York. After one evening surgery I received a message to go to the village inn. The landlord grunted that I should go "upstairs, fust on right and fust on left". I found myself facing a bedroom door. Grasping the door handle, I struggled to hold up a rather heavy door which had come away from its hinges, and which I deposited against the bedroom wall.

In bed lay the landlord's sister, who was suffering from a fractured skull, having fallen down the stairs. The landlord vehemently rejected a suggestion that his sister would be better in hospital and said that a day and a night nurse should be brought in to look after her at home. After two or three days, I persuaded the old man to let his sister go into hospital, where the next day, dressed in the formal dress of those days — bowler hat, dark suit and black overcoat — I paid her a visit, being ushered into a side room.

On the next visit, the ward sister told me that when I left, the patient sat up in bed and remarked: "Wasn't it nice of the Archbishop to come to visit me!"

Doctor Riddolls

An old daleswoman was ill in bed. A neighbour visited her in the afternoon to see if she was all right. The old lady thought it was her son coming home from work and called out: "George, tha mun put t'brass under t'bed. Them wimmins comin' in toneet!"

Canon Eric Allen

A junior reporter in Batley called at a house in the town to get particulars about a man who had died. The widow was very friendly and asked if he would like to see the body.

Unable to refuse, he did so and feeling some comment was called for, expressed the view that he looked very peaceful. She examined the corpse closely and said: "Aye, he does an' all, doesn't he? But he always were a bit slow on the uptake, were Albert, so happen he hasn't tumbled to what's happened to him yet."

Derrick Boothroyd

CONVERSATION PIECES

Young men and women in their first year at college are frequently ignorant of the names of their own local government areas. The following conversation was overheard:

A frustrated office assistant was dealing with a young lady from the remoter regions. "But surely you know the name of your Education Committee."

"No, I don't."

"Don't you know your home authority?"

This brought a flash of understanding to the student: "Oh, yes," she said, "That's me mum."

Carl Willmott

A Yorkshireman was going form York to Liverpool. He arrived at York station booking office and asked for a single ticket to Liverpool. The booking clerk threw the man the ticket, saying: "Change at Leeds."

The Yorkshireman quickly replied: "Ah'll hev it noo, if yer dean't mind." And he held out his hand for the change.

A Yorkshire farmer travelled by rail with his young son, who was a big lad. The farmer bought a whole ticket for himself and a half ticket for his son. The ticket collector accepted the farmer's tickets but claimed that the son was too old to qualify for half fare. The farmer quickly replied: "That's thy fault. He wor nobbut a lad when he left York."

Sydney Martin

A city motorist stopped on Blakey Ridge and asked an old shepherd the way to Rosedale Abbey. He was told there was a signpost half a mile down the road. The motorist said, teasingly, "But, my good man, what if I cannot read?" The shepherd replied: "It should just suit thi; there's nowt on it."

John E King

Two old Bilsdale residents were talking in the local pub. One was remarking on his recent dismissal from his job on the council roadways. He said: "I dean't knaw why a gat sack, a nivver did nowt." The other replied: "That's why."

Kenneth G Cook

A farmer named Swan lived in the village of Askham just outside York. When a visitor from the south saw a young lad driving some ducks along the street, he asked: "Whose ducks are they?" The boy replied, "Them's Swan's." "No, they're not," said the visitor, "where do they come from?" The boy simply replied: "Askham."

Stanley Bond

A number of farmers in the Dales pub were discussing the merits of their sheepdogs. Overhearing their conversation, and interested visitor — with a small corgi at his feet — invited opinions on that particular breed and wondered if it could ever be trained to handle sheep.

"Nay," commented the farmer, adding after a characteristic Yorkshire pause, "bit it might be right for rounding up a flock of hamsters."

Geoffrey N Wright

A Yorkshire village was two miles from the nearest railway station and had only one bus a day. A farmer asked his neighbour who was going that way with a pony and trap if he would ask if a parcel was waiting for him in the Parcel Office. "Of course I will," said the neighbour. In the evening when he returned, he just yelled out as he passed the farmer: "Yes, its here alreet."

Charlie Emett

AS SHE IS SPOKE

At a meeting of Yorkshiremen in Birmingham some years ago one man remarked how well he knew the County of Broad Acres and especially Ilkley.

A hitherto unobserved man in a corner piped up: "Tha'll knaw Ben Rhyddin' then!"

Flummoxed, he replied, "Well, Ah didn't knaw Ben so weel as 'is other brothers."

RH

There used to be an old market woman in Leeds market with a fine flow of dialect.

She once apologised for keeping a customer waiting because she was having her "minnin-on". When the customer asked what that was the old woman was surprised there were folk about that didn't understand plain English.

"Minnin-on?" she declared. "Well, it's just a bite o' summa to keep thi i'toit till tha gets roast beef and Yorksher. That's what minnin-on is."

J Wormald

During the last war a German plane was shot down, crashing in a field near a village in Holderness. A shocked and bleeding crew member crawled out of the wrecked plane, to be confronted by a grim-looking Yorkshire farmhand.

The German indicated he was wounded, hoping for sympathy.

The response was pointed and brief. The farmhand replied (in broad East Riding dialect): "Well! Tho shun't a cum!"

Wm Y Yoldsworth

Yorkshireman: "I think it's going to rain."
Staffordshireman: "Dost?"
Yorkshireman: "No, watter."

Rev J H Stringer

Travelling homeward on a bus over the Wolds was a teenage in uniform, obviously a member of the local Grammar School Cadet Force. He was smaller than average.

A young schoolboy sat staring at the diminutive soldier with great interest. When he alighted at a wayside farm, the boy

urned to his mother and remarked:

"Ee must 'a bin teeaned off t'nest ower seean!"

D H Whittaker

Old Johnny of Coverdale, long since dead, had a remarkable magination and was a grand story teller.

One tale was of Queen Victoria coming up to Middleham. ohnny (he declared) met her at Leyburn when her train came in.

The old Queen said: "Reach down that lile poke from t'rack, ohnny. It's a present for thee. We've been killing pigs at Windsor and I've brought thee some chitterlings."

E Winthrop-Young

"Nah, remember to do tha kerb drill," said the small boy nstructing his smaller companion, "or, (rolling his eyes) tha'll end up potted meeaht."

RH

A neighbour asked to use my telephone. The conversation fter dialling was as follows:

"Hello, is that thee? Aye, this is me. Tha knaws that theer I were tellin' thee abaht? Well, I've gitten it. I'll see thee toneet."

JW

Tom, who gained the coveted honour in Mesopotamia in World War One, was born this side of Oldham, at Springhead; and that makes him a Yorkshireman. But his twang at the time could have misled anybody into thinking that he was a "Lanky".

When he left for a Midland town his twang was noticed by Lancastrians there and they invited him to join their society.

"But I'm a Yorkshireman," he protested. "It doesn't matter," came the reply. "You talk like one of us. Besides t'treasurer's job's open and we've nobody we can trust wi' t'brass."

Samuel Cheesbrough

During the last war, in a unit of Royal Marines were two "Yorkies". One who spoke good English acted as interpreter to the other who spoke a rich Dewsbury dialect.

One day when "Dewsbury" had been giving voice, a listener said: "Yorkie, if you call a hole an 'oil, what do you say for oil?"

Like lightning came the answer: "Grease."

Arthur Smith

A Yorkshire farmer's wife, mother of six-year-old boy twins, gave birth to another son. The twins were invited to inspect.

After a long silence mother said: "Have yer nowt to say to yer new brother?"

"Aye," one child replied, "wheerst t'other?"

F P Hargreaves

A small child, out on an errand, damaged her hand in a garden gate latch. When she returned home, her mother asked: "Did you cry?" The child replied: "No, there was nobody there."

Wm A Jagger

This is a definition of a hill from my mother's remembrance of her schooldays in Bradford 70 years ago: "A gert lump o' muck, slantin' up straight."

F M Garth

A loquacious witness in a Leeds court was told by the magistrate to be a little more terse in his evidence.

"I suppose you know what terse means?"

"Course I do. It's t'first coach at a funeral!"

J Irwin